RECLAIM YOUR REMOTE

YWJ PUBLISHING

RECLAIM YOUR REMOTE

The ART Method for Letting Go of What You Can't Control and Taking Ownership of What You Can

Yvette W. Johnson, Ed.D.

Copyright

Reclaim Your Remote: The ART Method for Letting Go of What You Can't Control and Taking Ownership of What You Can

Published by: YWJ PUBLISHING
Website: ywjohnson.com

Library of Congress Control Number (LCCN): 2026914944
ISBN: 979-8-9965294-1-4

This book is intended for educational and personal-development purposes. It is not a substitute for psychotherapy, medical care, legal advice, crisis intervention, or individualized professional guidance. The principles in this book should never be used to excuse abuse, ignore danger, abandon a child or dependent adult, avoid a legal or professional duty, or remain silent when safety is at risk. In urgent or unsafe situations, seek appropriate professional and emergency support.

Some examples in this book are composites created to illustrate common patterns.

Contents

Introduction

Stop Carrying What Was Never Yours

What if the reason you are exhausted is not simply that life is hard?

What if you are exhausted because you have been carrying responsibilities that were never yours to begin with?

For a long time, I believed caring more was always the answer. When someone I loved was struggling, I worried harder. When someone made a decision I thought would hurt them, I explained more. When a relationship felt uncertain, I worked overtime to stabilize it. When someone was disappointed, I searched for what I could do to make the discomfort go away.

From the outside, this looked loving. Responsible. Strong.

Inside, it felt like living on call for everybody else's life.

I was not merely noticing other people's emotions; I was organizing myself around them. I was not simply offering support; I was measuring my peace by whether they accepted it. I was not only loving people; I was quietly assuming that love made me responsible for their choices, their reactions, their healing, and their outcomes.

Somewhere along the way, I stopped caring and started carrying.

There is a difference.

Caring says, "I am here with you."

Carrying says, "Your life is now my assignment."

Caring offers help.

Carrying cannot rest until the help is received, appreciated, and followed.

Caring respects another person's agency.

Carrying becomes anxious when that person chooses differently.

Caring is love with open hands.

Carrying is love clenched into a fist.

You may know this kind of exhaustion. It is the fatigue of replaying a conversation long after the other person has moved on. It is checking your phone because somebody's silence feels like a verdict. It is losing sleep over an adult who refuses your advice. It is saying yes while resentment rises in your chest. It is trying to prevent every mistake, smooth every conflict, anticipate every reaction, and make everyone understand.

It is a heavy way to live.

And because it often begins with good intentions, it can be difficult to recognize.

The Remote-Control Moment

Imagine that your life came with a remote control.

Not a magical device that keeps pain away. Not a button that makes other people behave. A remote that represents the authority you have over your attention, your response, your boundaries, your choices, and the meaning you assign to what happens.

Now imagine handing it to someone else.

A critical comment presses REWIND, and you replay it for three days.

A family member's mood turns the VOLUME up on your anxiety.

A friend's disapproval hits MUTE on your confidence.

A former partner presses PAUSE, and your life waits for closure that may never come.

A social media audience controls the channel, and your identity changes with every reaction.

The remote did not leave your hands all at once. It moved gradually—one reaction, one fear, one unspoken agreement at a time.

That is why the transfer can feel normal.

You tell yourself you are just being thoughtful. You are just trying to keep the peace. You are just making sure everyone is okay. You are just helping.

Yet the evidence is in your emotional life: someone else's behavior has become the deciding vote on whether you get to feel settled, confident, or free.

The central truth of this book is simple:

> *Other people can affect you without being allowed to direct you.*

You are human. You will feel hurt, disappointed, angry, afraid, and confused. Reclaiming your remote does not mean becoming emotionless. It means refusing to let a feeling, a person, or a circumstance become the permanent operator of your life.

The goal is not emotional control in the sense of never feeling. The goal is emotional leadership—the ability to feel honestly and still choose deliberately.

What You Can and Cannot Control

You cannot control whether someone agrees with you.

You cannot control whether an adult learns the lesson you wish they would learn.

You cannot control whether a relationship becomes what you hoped it would become.

You cannot control another person's honesty, maturity, effort, timing, or willingness to change.

You cannot control every outcome, prevent every loss, or guarantee that your best intentions will be understood.

That truth can feel frightening because control often masquerades as safety. We imagine that if we can manage enough people and predict enough outcomes, we can protect ourselves from pain.

But false control does not create safety. It creates vigilance.

It keeps your mind scanning, planning, correcting, rehearsing, and bracing. It makes rest feel irresponsible. It turns love into labor and relationships into projects.

The way back is not to care less. It is to become clear about what belongs to you.

Your response belongs to you.

Your values belong to you.

Your boundaries belong to you.

Your decisions belong to you.

Your healing belongs to you.

Your future belongs to you.

This is where the ART Method begins.

The ART Method

ART stands for:

Accept what you cannot control.

Release what does not belong to you.

Take Ownership of what does.

The order matters.

Acceptance brings you into contact with reality.

Release separates love from over-responsibility.

Ownership turns your attention toward meaningful action.

Without acceptance, you fight facts.

Without release, you carry people.

Without ownership, letting go can become avoidance.

ART is not passive. It is not indifference. It is not a permission slip for people to mistreat you. It is a disciplined way of asking, "What is true? What is mine? What will I do next?"

That final question is where your life changes.

A Necessary Distinction

There are times when action is required. If a child is unsafe, if someone is being abused, if a person is in immediate danger, if you hold a professional or legal duty, or if silence would enable serious harm, reclaiming your remote may mean speaking, reporting, intervening, leaving, documenting, or seeking help.

Release does not mean looking away.

Acceptance does not mean approval.

Ownership does not mean blaming yourself for what someone else did.

Boundaries do not mean punishment.

Peace does not require passivity.

This book is about wise responsibility, not less responsibility, and not responsibility for everyone. It is about putting responsibility where it belongs.

What This Book Will Help You Do

In the chapters ahead, you will learn how to identify the people, outcomes, and expectations that have been operating your emotional life. You will learn the difference between influence and control, between supporting and rescuing, between responsibility and blame, and between a boundary and a threat.

You will practice using ART in relationships, family conflict, workplace stress, criticism, people-pleasing, and moments of uncertainty. You will receive reflection questions, scripts, and short

Remote Resets that can be used in real time—not only when life is calm, but when your heart is racing and your old patterns are calling.

My hope is not that you finish this book feeling inspired for a day.

My hope is that you recognize the remote every time it begins to leave your hands.

That you pause before chasing approval.

That you stop confusing anxiety with responsibility.

That you can love people deeply without trying to live their lives for them.

That you can tell the truth without controlling the response.

That you can set a boundary without writing a closing argument.

That you can experience disappointment without surrendering your direction.

You do not need to become cold to become free.

You do not need to stop caring.

You need to stop carrying what love never asked you to carry.

The remote belongs in your hands.

Let us begin.

How to Use This Book

Do not rush through this book looking for the one sentence that will make every difficult person easier.

That sentence does not exist.

Instead, read with one relationship, one recurring stressor, or one area of emotional exhaustion in mind. Let the ideas become specific.

When a question makes you defensive, pause there. Defensiveness often protects a belief, role, or fear that deserves attention.

When a sentence brings relief, ask why. Relief may reveal a responsibility you are ready to return to its rightful owner.

When a boundary script sounds impossible, do not dismiss it. Ask what you believe would happen if you used it.

Keep a notebook nearby and make three columns:

What is true. Record facts and patterns you are ready to acknowledge.

What is not mine. Record choices, reactions, feelings, and outcomes you have been carrying for others.

What is mine. Record your values, boundaries, repairs, decisions, and next steps.

You may move through the book in order, or return to the chapter that matches the moment you are living. The ART Method is designed for repetition. Each time you apply it, you will see something new because you will be bringing a different situation—and a more honest version of yourself—to the questions.

Most important, do not turn this book into another standard you must perform perfectly.

You are not failing when you feel deeply.

You are not failing when an old pattern returns.

You are not failing when a boundary is difficult.

You are practicing a new form of leadership.

The purpose is not to become invulnerable. It is to become less available for self-abandonment.

Chapter 1

Who's Holding Your Remote?

Picture an ordinary morning.

You wake up feeling steady. Then you see a message from your supervisor: "Can we talk today?" Nothing more. Your body tightens. Before your feet touch the floor, your mind has written three versions of a disaster.

You check social media. A post you were proud of received less response than you expected. The confidence you had when you created it begins to disappear.

A family member calls with a familiar crisis. You had plans for your day, but guilt immediately rearranges them.

Your partner seems quiet. Instead of asking one clear question and allowing space for an answer, you begin monitoring tone, facial expression, and movement. Their mood becomes the weather system inside your body.

By 9:00 a.m., four different people and one algorithm have had access to your remote.

None of them asked for it.

You handed it over through interpretation, fear, habit, and the belief that your peace must wait until everything around you feels settled.

The Invisible Transfer of Power

Most people do not consciously decide to make other people responsible for their emotional well-being. The transfer begins early and often makes sense at the time.

A child learns that approval brings connection and criticism creates distance. A teenager discovers that belonging can feel like survival. An adult begins tying confidence to promotions, relationships, productivity, appearance, income, and public response.

Little by little, emotional authority moves outward.

Peace depends on whether the relationship is going well.

Confidence depends on whether the decision is applauded.

Self-worth depends on being needed.

Rest depends on everyone else being okay.

The problem is not that approval feels good. It does. The problem begins when approval becomes necessary for you to remain anchored.

When another person's reaction becomes the evidence that you are worthy, wise, lovable, or safe, your confidence becomes rented property. It can be taken back at any time.

A compliment lifts you beyond proportion.

A criticism collapses you beyond reason.

A delayed reply feels personal.

A boundary from someone else feels like rejection.

A disagreement feels like a threat to the relationship.

This is emotional outsourcing: assigning another person the job of deciding how you will feel about yourself.

The Buttons Other People Learn to Press

Every remote has buttons, and over time you begin to notice which ones are most sensitive.

Approval. You feel secure when people agree with you and unsettled when they do not.

Guilt. Someone's disappointment can make you abandon a decision you know is right.

Urgency. Another person's crisis becomes your emergency, even when the pattern is chronic and the responsibility is theirs.

Rejection. You overexplain, overperform, or overgive to prevent distance.

Comparison. Someone else's success becomes evidence that you are behind.

Conflict. You say yes, remain silent, or accept disrespect because tension feels unbearable.

Rescue. You feel most valuable when somebody needs saving.

The person pressing the button is not always malicious. Sometimes they are simply behaving as they have always behaved. Sometimes they are expressing an emotion. Sometimes they are asking, and you are interpreting the request as a command.

The work is not merely identifying who presses your buttons. It is understanding why those buttons control so much.

People-Pleasing: Kindness With a Hidden Contract

People-pleasing often looks generous. It can sound gentle, dependable, and selfless.

But beneath many people-pleasing patterns is an unspoken contract:

I will keep you comfortable so that I can feel safe.

You may never say those words aloud. Yet the contract shapes your choices.

When they are happy, you feel successful.

When they are disappointed, you feel guilty.

When they approve, you relax.

When they resist, you question yourself.

That is not free generosity. It is giving with an emotional invoice attached.

Healthy kindness is chosen. People-pleasing is compelled.

Healthy kindness can tolerate a no. People-pleasing fears what the no will cost.

Healthy kindness does not require control over the recipient's reaction. People-pleasing keeps checking to make sure the offering produced approval.

People-pleasers often become emotional weather forecasters. They scan rooms, messages, and facial expressions for signs of trouble. They notice everybody's needs before their own. They prepare for reactions that have not happened. They adjust, soften, apologize, and explain—sometimes before anyone has asked them to.

This constant monitoring is exhausting because it gives you an impossible assignment: manage the internal world of everyone around you.

No one can succeed at that job.

Approval-Seeking: The Silent Thief of Self-Trust

Approval-seeking and people-pleasing are close relatives. People-pleasing attempts to prevent disapproval. Approval-seeking attempts to earn validation.

It asks:

Do they like me?

Did I make the right impression?

Do they agree with my decision?

Am I doing enough?

Am I enough?

Again, wanting encouragement is human. Needing every important decision to be endorsed is different.

Each time you distrust your own considered judgment until somebody else confirms it, you weaken the muscle of self-trust. You may collect opinions from five people and still feel uncertain because the real question is not, "What do they think?" The real question is, "Can I remain connected to myself when they think differently?"

Self-trust does not mean assuming you are always right. It means believing you can listen, learn, make a decision, and handle the outcome without surrendering your identity.

Who (or What) Has the Remote?

A person may be holding your remote, but so can an outcome.

Success can hold it.

Money can hold it.

A title can hold it.

A number on a scale can hold it.

A deadline, diagnosis, election, court decision, business launch, family image, or dream can hold it.

You know something has the remote when you tell yourself, "I cannot be okay unless this turns out the way I want."

Hope is healthy. Desire is healthy. Goals are healthy.

Emotional captivity begins when your entire sense of self becomes attached to an outcome you do not fully control.

You can work hard without making the result your identity.

You can pray without demanding a particular timeline.

You can love someone without making their growth the condition of your peace.

You can want reconciliation and still build a life if it does not come.

You can pursue a dream and survive a detour.

The remote stays with you when your desires are strong, but your identity is not hostage to them.

Four Ways We Hand Away the Remote

People surrender emotional authority in different ways. You may recognize yourself in more than one of these patterns.

The Mood Manager

The Mood Manager enters a room and immediately scans the emotional climate.

Who is quiet?

Who looks irritated?

Who needs encouragement?

What can be said—or avoided—to keep the atmosphere calm?

This sensitivity may have developed in a home where moods were unpredictable, conflict felt unsafe, or connection depended on keeping an important person pleased. As an adult, the Mood Manager can be thoughtful and emotionally perceptive. The difficulty comes when awareness becomes assignment.

The unspoken belief is: *If somebody is upset, I must have missed something or failed to do something.*

Reclaiming the remote means learning that you can notice an emotion without adopting it. You can ask one caring question and allow the answer to remain with the person who gives it.

The Fixer

The Fixer feels most valuable when there is a problem to solve.

They research, organize, advise, call, pay, schedule, remind, and intervene. Their competence is real, and people may rely on it heavily.

The danger is that usefulness becomes identity. When no one needs help, the Fixer may feel unnecessary. When advice is ignored, the Fixer may feel rejected rather than merely disagreed with.

The unspoken belief is: *If I can solve this, I can keep everyone safe—and prove that I matter.*

Reclaiming the remote means asking whether support was requested and whether the proposed help strengthens the other person's capacity. The Fixer does not have to stop being gifted. The gift needs boundaries.

The Approval Earner

The Approval Earner performs for belonging.

They become the dependable employee, the low-maintenance friend, the agreeable family member, the person who anticipates what others want before anyone asks.

They may have impressive achievements and fragile self-trust at the same time. Every decision is run through an imaginary panel: Will they approve? Will they think I am selfish? Will they still respect me?

The unspoken belief is: *My place is secure only while I am pleasing, producing, or proving.*

Reclaiming the remote means making some decisions privately, tolerating the space before feedback arrives, and learning that disagreement does not automatically equal rejection.

The Outcome Chaser

The Outcome Chaser attaches peace to one specific result.

The relationship must work.

The child must choose wisely.

The business must succeed by a particular date.

The conversation must end with understanding.

Goals are healthy. The remote changes hands when a desired outcome becomes the only acceptable evidence that life is okay.

The unspoken belief is: *I cannot be at peace while the ending remains uncertain.*

Reclaiming the remote means pursuing goals with commitment while refusing to make identity, worth, or survival depend on a result you do not fully control.

Your Primary Pattern

Complete these sentences:

When someone is upset, I tend to...

When someone I love has a problem, I tend to...

When I fear disapproval, I tend to...

When an outcome is uncertain, I tend to...

The pattern that costs me the most peace is...

The need beneath that pattern may be...

The first new behavior I am willing to practice is...

Naming your pattern is not placing yourself in a box. It is finding the door.

The Remote Audit

Pause and answer honestly:

Who can ruin your day with a facial expression?

Whose approval are you still trying to earn?

Whose silence makes you abandon your self-respect?

Whose choices create the most anxiety in your life?

Who are you trying to fix, save, convince, or control?

What outcome have you made responsible for your happiness?

Where do you say yes because you are afraid of the reaction to no?

What do you repeatedly replay, amplify, or personalize?

These questions are not invitations to shame yourself. They are a way to locate the remote.

You cannot reclaim what you refuse to recognize.

The First Reclaiming

Reclaiming your remote rarely begins with a dramatic confrontation. It begins with a small internal shift:

"Their reaction is information. It is not instruction."

"Their disappointment is real. It is not automatically my responsibility."

"I can feel hurt without chasing."

"I can hear criticism without handing over my identity."

"I can care about this outcome without making it the ruler of my peace."

That is the beginning of emotional leadership.

Not denying what you feel.

Not controlling what they feel.

Choosing what happens next.

Remote Reset

When you feel your remote leaving your hands, pause and ask:

1. **What button was just pressed?** Approval, guilt, urgency, rejection, comparison, conflict, or rescue?
2. **What story am I telling myself?** Separate the facts from your interpretation.
3. **What choice would keep me aligned with my values?** Not comfortable, but aligned.

One Sentence to Carry

Other people may influence my emotions, but they do not get to direct my life.

Chapter 2

The Control Illusion

If Chapter 1 helped you identify who is holding your remote, this chapter asks a harder question:

Why did you hand it over?

Most controlling behavior does not begin with a desire to dominate. It begins with a desire to prevent pain.

You want certainty.

You want the person you love to be okay.

You want to avoid rejection, embarrassment, loss, conflict, or regret.

You want the plan to work because you are not sure you can handle what happens if it does not.

Control becomes the strategy you use to negotiate with uncertainty.

If I explain it perfectly, they will understand.

If I help enough, they will change.

If I anticipate every problem, nothing will go wrong.

If I make the right decision, nobody will be disappointed.

If I stay vigilant, I will not be blindsided.

The intention is protection.

The result is exhaustion.

Why Uncertainty Feels So Threatening

The human mind searches for patterns. It wants to predict what comes next. That ability is useful; it helps us prepare, learn, and survive.

But the same mind that plans wisely can also become trapped in the fantasy that enough thinking will eliminate uncertainty.

You rehearse conversations that have not happened.

You try to read motives you cannot verify.

You create backup plans for backup plans.

You offer advice nobody requested because watching another person choose feels intolerable.

You confuse mental activity with effective action.

Worry can feel productive because it creates the sensation that you are doing something. Often, you are repeatedly touching a problem you cannot solve.

The question is not whether uncertainty is comfortable. It is not.

The question is whether your attempt to remove uncertainty is costing you more than uncertainty itself.

Concern or Control?

Control often wears the clothes of concern.

"I am only trying to help."

"I know how this will end."

"Somebody has to tell them."

"I just want what is best."

Sometimes that is exactly what is happening. There are moments when guidance, protection, and intervention are appropriate.

The difference is found in what happens after you communicate.

Concern can offer wisdom and release the outcome.

Control must secure compliance.

Concern respects an adult's right to choose.

Control treats disagreement as disobedience.

Concern asks, "Would you like my thoughts?"

Control keeps talking after the answer is no.

Concern can stay connected without becoming responsible for the result.

Control cannot settle until the other person does what it believes is right.

A helpful question is: **Am I trying to contribute, or am I trying to guarantee?**

You can contribute care, information, resources, honesty, and support.

You cannot guarantee another person's decision, effort, healing, or outcome.

Influence Is Not Control

Influence is real and valuable. Parents influence children. Leaders influence teams. Partners influence each other. Friends influence friends.

Influence says, "Here is what I see."

Control says, "You must see it my way."

Influence says, "Here is what I can offer."

Control says, "You must use what I offered."

Influence invites.

Control insists.

Influence can survive a no.

Control experiences no as a threat.

This distinction protects relationships because autonomy matters. People are more likely to grow when they own the choice. Even wise advice can become ineffective when it is delivered as pressure.

Your goal is not to become silent. It is to speak clearly without making another person's response the measure of whether you get to be at peace.

The Frustration Trap

Much of frustration is created by an unspoken condition:

"I can feel better when they behave differently."

Your spouse must communicate the way you prefer.

Your adult child must make the decision you would make.

Your coworker must stop being difficult.

Your parent must finally acknowledge the past.

Your friend must recognize how much you have given.

You may have legitimate needs and reasonable expectations. Yet when your well-being is entirely postponed until another person changes, you enter the frustration trap.

You are waiting for a person you do not control to hand your life back to you.

The way out is not pretending the behavior does not matter. It is moving from demand to decision.

Demand: "They must change so I can be okay."

Decision: "This behavior matters, and I will choose my response."

That response might be a conversation, a boundary, a changed expectation, professional support, distance, documentation, forgiveness, or an ending.

The power is not in making them different.

The power is in becoming clear about what you will do with what is true.

How Control Creates Anxiety

When you assume responsibility for outcomes you do not control, your mind has no natural stopping point.

There is always another scenario to consider.

Another mistake to prevent.

Another message to send.

Another explanation to offer.

Another sign to analyze.

You become hypervigilant because you have accepted an assignment with no boundaries.

Anxiety grows when your circle of responsibility expands beyond your actual authority.

You are responsible for communicating honestly. You are not responsible for guaranteeing understanding.

You are responsible for parenting a minor with care and appropriate structure. You are not responsible for controlling every feeling or future choice that child will have.

You are responsible for leading with clarity. You are not responsible for making every employee enthusiastic.

You are responsible for apologizing when you cause harm. You are not responsible for forcing forgiveness.

When responsibility and authority do not match, distress rises. You are trying to answer for something you do not have the power to direct.

The Resentment Cycle

Control often produces resentment through a predictable sequence:

You overfunction.

You expect the effort to create change.

The other person continues choosing for themselves.

You feel unappreciated, used, or betrayed.

You think, "After everything I have done..."

The resentment is real, and it may reveal that you have given too much, communicated too little, or attached an unspoken expectation to your help.

This does not mean the other person has behaved well. It means you must examine the agreement you created without their participation.

A silent contract sounds like:

"I will rescue you, and in return you will become who I need you to become."

"I will avoid conflict, and in return you will never be upset with me."

"I will always be available, and in return you will value me."

"I will carry the family, and in return everyone will recognize my sacrifice."

When the other person violates a contract they never knew existed, bitterness grows.

Freedom requires making expectations visible, help voluntary, and limits honest.

The Four Control Strategies

Control does not always look forceful. Often it looks productive, caring, intelligent, or responsible. It helps to recognize the strategies beneath the surface.

Prediction

Prediction tries to remove uncertainty by thinking through every possible outcome.

You replay the meeting before it occurs. You imagine the objections. You prepare responses to conversations that may never happen. You monitor a loved one's tone for evidence of what comes next.

Planning is useful when it ends in preparation. Prediction becomes control when the mind keeps rehearsing after no additional action is available.

Ask: *Is this thought helping me prepare, or helping me pretend I can guarantee the future?*

Persuasion

Persuasion believes that one more explanation will create the desired choice.

You send another article. You restate the concern. You change the wording. You recruit someone else to reinforce the message.

Communication is necessary. Repeated persuasion becomes control when another person's no, difference, or delay is treated as evidence that you have not explained well enough.

Ask: *Have I communicated clearly—and am I now refusing to accept that the decision belongs to someone else?*

Prevention

Prevention attempts to remove every consequence before it arrives.

You cover the missed payment, make the excuse, complete the unfinished work, call ahead, smooth the conflict, or absorb the cost.

Prevention is appropriate when you have a genuine duty of care or safety is at stake. It becomes control when an able adult is repeatedly protected from the information their consequences would provide.

Ask: *Am I preventing harm, or preventing discomfort that may belong to growth?*

Perfection

Perfection tries to control criticism by becoming impossible to criticize.

You overprepare, overperform, and delay decisions until every variable feels managed. You believe that if you choose correctly enough, no one will be disappointed and nothing will go wrong.

Perfection is an impossible contract with reality. Excellent work can reduce preventable problems. It cannot purchase universal approval or immunity from loss.

Ask: *What would responsible and complete look like if perfect were no longer the requirement?*

The Fear Beneath Control

Under each strategy is often a fear:

If I cannot predict, I may be blindsided.

If I cannot persuade, I may be powerless.

If I cannot prevent, someone may suffer—and blame me.

If I am not perfect, I may be rejected.

The answer is not to mock the fear. It is to strengthen your confidence that you can respond to life without controlling every variable in advance.

Self-trust sounds like:

"I do not know exactly what will happen, but I will meet the truth when it arrives."

"I can communicate clearly without forcing agreement."

"I can allow appropriate consequences without withdrawing love."

"I can survive being imperfect and still act with integrity."

Three Circles of Responsibility

When a situation feels overwhelming, sort it into three circles.

Circle One: What I Control

My words.

My behavior.

My preparation.

My boundaries.

My effort.

My decision to stay, leave, speak, pause, document, forgive, or seek support.

Circle Two: What I Can Influence

A conversation.

A relationship climate.

A team's direction.

A loved one's access to information or resources.

The likelihood of a better outcome.

Influence matters, but it is not a guarantee.

Circle Three: What I Cannot Carry

Another adult's choices.

Another person's private thoughts.

The past.

The timing of someone else's growth.

Universal approval.

Every possible outcome.

The mistake is not caring about Circle Three. The mistake is building your home there.

When Releasing Control Is Not the Same as Doing Nothing

This point matters.

You should not "release" a situation that requires action simply because action is uncomfortable.

If someone is in danger, act.

If a child or dependent person needs protection, act.

If abuse, harassment, discrimination, fraud, or serious misconduct occurs, use the appropriate channels.

If your health requires attention, seek care.

If your values require a difficult conversation, have it.

The ART Method does not teach helplessness. It teaches accurate responsibility.

You cannot control the final outcome, but you may be responsible for your part.

Sometimes reclaiming your remote means letting go.

Sometimes it means standing up.

Wisdom is knowing the difference.

Remote Reset

Ask yourself:

1. **Am I contributing or trying to guarantee?**
2. **Which circle does this belong in: control, influence, or release?**
3. **What action is mine even if the outcome is not?**

One Sentence to Carry

Peace does not come from controlling more; it comes from carrying only what is truly mine.

Chapter 3

The ART Method: Your Freedom Formula

By now, you have seen the pattern.

You hand away your remote when another person's behavior becomes the condition of your peace. You reach for control when uncertainty feels unbearable. You overthink, overfunction, overexplain, and overcarry because doing something feels safer than admitting what you cannot direct.

The question is: What do you do instead?

You use ART.

Accept. Release. Take Ownership.

These are not three inspirational words. They are a sequence for returning to reality, responsibility, and choice.

ART helps you answer three questions:

What is true?

What is not mine?

What will I do?

That is the entire movement from emotional captivity to emotional leadership.

Step One: Accept What You Cannot Control

Acceptance means acknowledging reality as it exists right now.

Not as it should be.

Not as it used to be.

Not as you hoped it would become.

As it is.

Acceptance may sound like:

"This person does not want the help I am offering."

"The relationship has changed."

"My supervisor gave me critical feedback."

"My adult child made a choice I would not have made."

"I cannot make this person tell the truth."

"The opportunity is no longer available."

"I am hurt."

Acceptance is not approval, agreement, forgiveness, reconciliation, or surrender. It is the end of arguing with the fact that something is already true.

You cannot make a wise decision from a reality you refuse to name.

Step Two: Release What Does Not Belong to You

Once you acknowledge what is true, you decide what you will no longer carry.

Release may mean letting go of responsibility for another adult's choices.

It may mean releasing the need to be understood by someone committed to misunderstanding you.

It may mean releasing the fantasy that one more explanation will produce a different character.

It may mean releasing guilt for setting a healthy limit.

It may mean releasing an outcome while continuing to pursue a goal.

It may mean grieving the relationship you wanted so you can respond to the relationship you actually have.

Release is not careless. It is clarifying.

You are not saying, "It does not matter."

You are saying, "It matters, and I will not carry what I cannot control."

For readers whose faith is central, release may also mean entrusting what you cannot control to God rather than repeatedly trying to occupy a role that was never yours.

Step Three: Take Ownership of What Does

ART does not end with letting go.

This is what keeps the method from becoming passive.

Ownership asks:

What is my next right action?

What boundary is needed?

What conversation do I need to have?

What apology do I owe?

What support should I seek?

What pattern must I stop participating in?

What decision aligns with my values?

How will I care for my emotional and physical well-being?

Ownership moves your focus from their behavior to your leadership.

It does not blame you for what happened. It refuses to leave your future entirely in the hands of what happened.

Why the Sequence Matters

Each part of ART corrects a common mistake.

Acceptance without release becomes resignation. You see reality but continue carrying it as though you are responsible for changing it.

Release without ownership becomes avoidance. You detach, disappear, or call inaction peace.

Ownership without acceptance becomes control. You take action based on the reality you wish existed instead of the one in front of you.

The full sequence creates balance.

Accept the facts.

Release false responsibility.

Own your response.

ART in a Difficult Conversation

Imagine that a close friend has repeatedly canceled plans at the last minute.

Your old pattern might be to say nothing, act as if it is fine, then complain to someone else. Or you may send an angry message designed to make the friend feel as disappointed as you do.

ART offers another path.

Accept: "This has happened several times, and it is affecting my trust."

Release: "I cannot force my friend to value plans the way I do, and I do not need to prove that my feelings are reasonable."

Take Ownership: "I will address the pattern directly and make future plans differently."

A script might be:

> *"I value our friendship, and repeated last-minute cancellations have been difficult for me. Going forward, I am going to stop rearranging important commitments unless plans are confirmed. I would still like to spend time together, and I need a more reliable way of planning."*

You are not controlling your friend's response. You are leading your participation.

ART With an Adult Child

An adult child is making a financial decision you believe is unwise.

Accept: "They are an adult, and this is their decision."

Release: "I am not responsible for preventing every consequence."

Take Ownership: "I can offer my perspective once, clarify what financial help I will or will not provide, and remain loving without financing a pattern I do not support."

A script might be:

> *"I love you, and I trust that the decision is yours. I am willing to share what I see if you want my perspective. I also need to be clear that I will not be able to cover the cost if this choice creates a shortfall."*

That is care without carrying.

ART at Work

A colleague criticizes your proposal in a meeting.

Accept: "The criticism happened, and I feel embarrassed."

Release: "I cannot control the colleague's tone or make everyone view me positively."

Take Ownership: "I will evaluate the substance, ask a clarifying question, improve what is useful, and address disrespect privately if needed."

A script might be:

> *"I want to understand the concern. Which part of the proposal do you believe creates the greatest risk? We can address the substance now, and I would also like to speak privately about how the feedback was delivered."*

Ownership is neither collapse nor attack. It is grounded action.

ART in One Complete Moment

Consider this composite example.

Monica has become the person everyone in her family calls when something goes wrong. She is competent, generous, and proud that her adult children trust her. Her son calls to say he is behind on rent again. He explains that work has been inconsistent and asks whether she can cover the balance.

Monica's body reacts before her mind catches up. Her chest tightens. She begins calculating which bill she can delay. She also feels anger because this is the third crisis in six months.

Her usual pattern is immediate rescue followed by private resentment.

This time, she pauses and applies ART.

Accept

She separates the facts from the fear.

The fact is that her adult son is behind on rent.

The fact is that he has asked her for money.

The fact is that she has helped twice before and the underlying pattern has not changed.

The fear is that he will lose housing, become angry with her, or believe she is a bad mother if she does not pay.

Acceptance does not tell Monica what answer to give. It prevents fear from pretending to be fact.

Release

Monica releases responsibility for proving her love through immediate payment.

She releases the belief that her son's disappointment would mean she had failed him.

She releases the fantasy that another rescue will guarantee stability.

She does not release compassion. She does not release the duty to respond honestly. She releases the outcome she cannot guarantee.

Take Ownership

Monica considers her actual capacity and values.

She decides she will not pay the entire balance. She is willing to contribute a smaller one-time amount directly to the landlord if her son meets with a housing counselor, creates a written plan, and identifies what he will change before the next payment is due.

She also decides that she will not discuss the request while being insulted or pressured.

Her response is:

"I love you, and I understand that this is frightening. I am not able to cover the full rent. I can contribute $___ directly to the landlord one time, and I am willing to help you identify local support and create a plan. I understand that this may not be the answer you wanted. It is what I can responsibly offer."

Her son is disappointed. He accuses her of not understanding.

The old Monica would treat that emotion as an emergency and reverse her decision.

The new Monica reminds herself:

His disappointment is real.

It is not automatically my responsibility to remove.

I can remain loving while my limit remains true.

ART does not guarantee a pleasant conversation. It creates an honest one.

What ART Changed

The method did not decide for Monica. It helped her make the decision from reality instead of panic.

It separated love from rescue.

It allowed her son's feelings to exist without becoming the operator of her finances.

It replaced an automatic pattern with a deliberate response.

This is how ART works in real life. The freedom is not always in getting the outcome you want. Sometimes it is in respecting the decision you made from truth.

The Ninety-Second ART Practice

When emotions are high, do not demand an immediate perfect response from yourself. Use ninety seconds to create space.

Pause. Put both feet on the floor. Exhale longer than you inhale. Do not send the message yet.

Name. Say what is true without exaggeration: "I feel rejected." "I am angry." "I am afraid this will not work."

Sort. Identify what is yours and what is not.

Choose. Decide the smallest action that reflects your values.

The goal is not to feel nothing. It is to prevent a temporary feeling from making a permanent decision.

The ART Card

Keep these questions where you can see them:

ACCEPT

What is true right now?

What am I resisting?

What fact remains true even if I dislike it?

RELEASE

What am I carrying that does not belong to me?

Whose emotion, choice, lesson, or outcome have I adopted?

What need for approval or certainty can I loosen?

TAKE OWNERSHIP

What is my next right action?

What boundary, conversation, apology, decision, or support is mine?

What choice keeps the remote in my hands?

ART Is a Practice, Not a Personality

You will not use ART perfectly.

There will be days when you catch yourself after the argument, after the rescuing, after the overexplaining, after you have spent an hour replaying something that deserved five minutes.

That does not mean the method failed.

The moment you notice is the moment you can return.

Freedom is not never handing away the remote.

Freedom is knowing how to take it back.

Remote Reset

Use one line for each step:

Accept: The truth is...

Release: I am no longer responsible for...

Take Ownership: My next right action is...

One Sentence to Carry

ART turns "Why are they doing this?" into "What is true, what is mine, and what will I do next?"

Chapter 4

Accept What Is

Acceptance is where freedom begins, and it is often where people resist the hardest.

We do not resist reality because we are foolish. We resist because reality can hurt.

The relationship ended.

The apology did not come.

The person you love is making a choice you would not make.

The workplace is not as fair as you believed it should be.

The opportunity passed.

The diagnosis is real.

The family member you keep waiting on may never become the person you need them to be.

Acceptance asks you to stop negotiating with what has already revealed itself.

That can feel cruel at first. In truth, it is one of the kindest things you can do for yourself.

Acceptance Is Not Approval

Acceptance is not saying, "This is good."

It is saying, "This is true."

You can accept that someone lied without approving of dishonesty.

You can accept that a relationship has become unhealthy without pretending the history meant nothing.

You can accept that another adult has the right to choose without believing the choice is wise.

You can accept that a system is unfair while still working to change it.

Acceptance does not cancel action. It makes wise action possible.

Before acceptance, you react to the reality you wish existed.

After acceptance, you respond to the reality that is actually in front of you.

That distinction can save years.

The Three Stories We Tell About Reality

When something painful happens, the mind often creates three layers:

The fact: What happened.

The interpretation: What you believe it means.

The prediction: What you fear will happen next.

Suppose a friend does not return your call.

The fact is: *My friend has not called me back.*

The interpretation may be: *She does not value me. or She does not want to talk to me.*

The prediction may be: *I am going to lose this friendship, and I always lose people.*

Only the first sentence is verified.

Your interpretation may eventually prove accurate, but it is not yet a fact. Your prediction may express a real fear, but it is not a certainty.

Emotional leadership begins by separating what happened from the story that immediately formed around it.

Ask:

What do I know?

What am I assuming?

What am I afraid this means?

What information do I still need?

This is not about talking yourself out of your instincts. It is about giving yourself enough clarity to use them wisely.

Grieving the Version You Hoped For

Sometimes the hardest thing to accept is not what happened. It is what will not happen.

You are not only grieving the relationship you have. You are grieving the relationship you kept believing was possible.

You are not only disappointed in a decision. You are releasing the future you imagined that decision would create.

You are not merely accepting a person's limitations. You are grieving the version of them you kept waiting to meet.

That grief deserves honesty.

Many people remain trapped because they think acceptance should make them feel peaceful immediately. It may not. Acceptance can feel like sadness before it feels like relief.

The first gift of acceptance is not happiness.

It is clarity.

Clarity tells you where you are.

Then grief helps you release where you thought you would be.

Only after that can peace begin to grow.

Stop Arguing With the Evidence

A painful pattern does not become less real because there were good moments between the painful ones.

Potential is not the same as pattern.

An apology is not the same as repair.

A promise is not the same as practice.

Intent is not the same as impact.

One of the most expensive emotional habits is repeatedly giving greater authority to a person's words than to their consistent behavior.

You do not have to label someone as bad in order to admit that their pattern is harmful to you.

You do not have to prove malicious intent before you respond to repeated impact.

You do not have to wait until a situation becomes unbearable before you call it unsustainable.

Acceptance asks a sober question:

What has this person, relationship, or situation consistently shown me?

Then it asks you to believe the evidence.

Acceptance Without Helplessness

There is a difference between accepting what you cannot control and deciding you have no choices.

You may not control whether your employer values your contribution. You can document your work, speak up, seek support, or explore another position.

You may not control whether a family member respects your boundary. You can change the access they have to you.

You may not control whether someone apologizes. You can decide what healing looks like without their participation.

You may not control the past. You can choose what the past is allowed to teach, and what it is no longer allowed to run.

Acceptance removes fantasy, not agency.

It says, "I will stop spending my power denying this reality so I can use my power responding to it."

Acceptance and Ambiguous Loss

Some losses have no clean ending.

A parent is alive but emotionally unavailable.

A marriage continues, but the intimacy you hoped for has not returned.

An adult child is present but distant.

A friendship fades without a final conversation.

A loved one changes through illness, addiction, or cognitive decline.

This is sometimes called ambiguous loss: the person or relationship is both present and absent in important ways. The lack of a clear ending can keep hope and grief locked in the same room.

You may ask:

Am I allowed to grieve when the person is still here?

Am I giving up too soon?

What if things change after I accept that they may not?

Acceptance does not require you to predict the future. It allows you to stop postponing your life while waiting for one preferred version of the future.

You can leave room for change without building your home in the waiting room.

You can say:

"I remain open to healthy repair, and I will make decisions based on the pattern that exists now."

"I can love this person and grieve what they are unable to offer."

"I will not deny today's reality in order to protect tomorrow's possibility."

Ambiguous loss often needs ritual because there may be no public event that acknowledges it. Write the letter you may never send. Name what you hoped for. Mark the ending of an expectation. Share the grief with someone who will not rush you toward false closure.

You do not have to turn hope off.

You do have to stop using hope to silence evidence.

The Cost of Refusing Reality

Resistance does more than preserve hope. It consumes attention.

You keep reviewing old conversations for a missing clue.

You treat every small improvement as proof that the entire pattern has changed.

You postpone boundaries because the next week may be different.

You remain emotionally unavailable to the life in front of you because so much energy is invested in the life you planned.

Acceptance returns that energy.

It gives you permission to build with what is available, not only mourn what is absent.

When Acceptance Requires Help

Some realities are too heavy to process alone.

Trauma, abuse, grief, betrayal, addiction, financial crisis, discrimination, and serious mental-health concerns may require support beyond self-reflection. Reclaiming your remote does not mean handling everything privately. Asking for qualified help is an act of ownership. Therapy can often be a very beneficial step for many people.

Acceptance should never be used to pressure someone to tolerate danger, remain silent, reconcile prematurely, or bypass grief. Safety comes before relational comfort. Accountability matters. Legal and professional obligations still apply.

Healthy acceptance tells the truth about harm and then chooses the safest, wisest next step available.

Practice: Fact, Story, Fear, Choice

Choose one situation that repeatedly activates you. Divide a page into four sections.

FACT

Write only what a camera could record or a neutral observer could verify.

Avoid words such as *always, never, obviously,* and *does not care* unless they describe verified frequency or a direct statement.

STORY

Write what you believe the facts mean.

Do you believe the person is rejecting you, disrespecting you, replacing you, or proving that you are not enough?

The story may contain truth. The purpose is not to dismiss it. The purpose is to see it.

FEAR

Write the outcome your mind is trying to prevent.

What are you afraid will happen next?

What are you afraid this says about you?

What earlier experience does the situation resemble?

CHOICE

Write the action that remains available even if your story or fear proves true.

What question can you ask?

What boundary can you set?

What support can you seek?

What decision can you postpone until you have more information?

What truth can you survive?

This practice does not guarantee that your fear is unfounded. It proves that fear is not the only voice available when you decide what to do.

The Acceptance Inventory

Complete these sentences without explaining, defending, or minimizing:

The reality I keep resisting is...

The pattern I keep calling a one-time incident is...

The person I keep trying to turn into someone else is...

The ending I have not fully grieved is...

The truth my body seems to know before my mind admits it is...

The fact I need to separate from my interpretation is...

The choice that becomes available once I accept what is true is...

Remote Reset

Write three lines:

The fact is: ...

The story I am telling is: ...

The wisest next step is: ...

One Sentence to Carry

Acceptance does not ask you to like reality; it gives you the clarity to lead yourself within it.

Chapter 5

Release What Isn't Yours

Once you accept reality, the next question is not, "How can I make this different?"

It is, "What am I carrying that does not belong to me?"

Many of us carry emotional luggage so long that we stop noticing the weight.

A parent's expectations.

A partner's happiness.

An adult child's consequences.

A friend's crisis.

A coworker's lack of preparation.

A family's image.

A community's opinion.

At first, carrying feels useful. It gives you something to do when uncertainty makes you feel powerless. Over time, it becomes an identity: the fixer, the strong one, the peacemaker, the dependable one, the person who can always be counted on.

Those roles may be honorable. They become harmful when your worth depends on performing them without limits.

Caring and Carrying Are Not the Same

Caring says, "I love you, and I believe your life belongs to you."

Carrying says, "I love you, so I must prevent your discomfort, absorb your consequences, and keep your life from falling apart."

Caring can listen without taking over.

Carrying feels compelled to produce an outcome.

Caring asks what support would be helpful.

Carrying assumes responsibility before it is requested.

Caring respects capacity—yours and theirs.

Carrying gives until resentment becomes the receipt.

You can be compassionate without becoming consumed.

You can be available without being endlessly accessible.

You can support someone and still leave the decision in their hands.

The Silent Contract

Overfunctioning often contains an unspoken contract:

I will do more than my share, and in return you will become who I need you to be.

You may never say it aloud. The contract reveals itself through resentment.

"After everything I have done..."

"Why do I care more than they do?"

"I have tried so hard, and nothing changes."

Resentment does not always mean you are selfish. Sometimes it means you have been giving with expectations you did not name, to someone who never agreed to meet them.

Release begins by canceling the silent contract.

You give because the choice aligns with your values, not because it guarantees another person's transformation.

You help within healthy limits, not as a down payment on loyalty.

You speak truth because truth matters, not because you can force someone to accept it.

Rescuing Can Interrupt Growth

Rescuing is different from helping.

Helping strengthens a person's ability to carry their own life.

Rescuing repeatedly removes the natural responsibility connected to their choices.

Helping asks, "What can you do, and what support do you need?"

Rescuing says, "Move aside. I will do it for you."

Sometimes immediate rescue is necessary. Children, dependent adults, emergencies, illness, disability, and safety concerns may create real duties of care. Wisdom considers context.

But in ordinary adult relationships, constant rescue can communicate a message you never intended:

I do not trust you to face your own life.

Allowing someone to struggle is not always abandonment. Sometimes it is respect.

Consequences can teach what your repeated explanations cannot.

Experience can create a readiness that advice could not manufacture.

Love does not require you to stand between an able adult and every lesson their life is trying to teach them.

Release the Need to Be Understood

One of the heaviest burdens is the need to make everyone understand your motives.

You explain the boundary again.

You provide more context.

You revise the text message.

You present evidence.

You rehearse the conversation.

You hope that one perfect sentence will make another person see your heart accurately.

Clear communication matters. Endless explanation is different.

Some people misunderstand because they lack information. Others misunderstand because your decision inconveniences them. More explanation will not solve a conflict rooted in entitlement.

You are responsible for being honest, respectful, and clear.

You are not responsible for controlling the conclusion another person reaches about you.

At some point, peace sounds like:

"I have explained my decision. I understand that you disagree. My decision remains the same."

Release Other People's Emotions

You can care that someone is disappointed without treating their disappointment as proof you did something wrong.

You can feel compassion for someone's anger without volunteering to become its target.

You can acknowledge sadness without reversing a healthy decision simply to make the sadness disappear.

Another person's emotion is information. It is not always instruction.

People are allowed to have feelings about your choices.

You are allowed to have choices they have feelings about.

This is especially difficult for people-pleasers because discomfort feels like danger. When somebody becomes unhappy, the nervous system may rush to restore connection at any cost.

Pause.

Ask whether repair is needed—or whether discomfort simply needs room to exist.

Not every uncomfortable emotion is a problem to solve.

A Four-Part Help Test

Before stepping in, ask:

Was help requested?

Unrequested help can become control wearing a generous face.

Do I have the capacity?

A loving yes that destroys your health, finances, or stability may not be a wise yes.

Will my help strengthen or replace responsibility?

Support should not repeatedly make another person's avoidance possible.

Can I give without controlling the outcome?

If your peace depends on them using the help exactly as you prescribe, the gift may contain a hidden demand.

You do not have to say no to every request. You do need to know what your yes means.

When Helping Becomes an Identity

Some people do not merely help. They know themselves through helping.

They are the one who remembers birthdays, checks on everyone, finds the solution, hosts the gathering, pays the shortfall, and keeps the family connected. Others may praise this role, depend on it, and resist any change to it.

The role can become so central that limits feel like an identity crisis.

If I am not the strong one, who am I?

If people stop needing me, will they still choose me?

If I let them handle it, what value do I bring?

If I rest, will everything fall apart?

These questions deserve compassion. They reveal that overfunctioning may provide rewards alongside exhaustion.

It may provide certainty.

It may protect you from examining your own unmet needs.

It may create closeness without requiring vulnerability because you can give help instead of asking for it.

It may provide moral authority: the person who sacrifices most can feel entitled to decide most.

It may keep you indispensable in relationships where you are not sure you feel loved.

Release becomes sustainable only when you build an identity larger than usefulness.

You are not valuable only when solving.

You are not lovable only when giving.

You are not safe only when needed.

You are allowed to be known for your presence, humor, ideas, tenderness, creativity, wisdom, faith, curiosity, and humanity—not merely your capacity to absorb a crisis.

From Rescuer to Resource

A rescuer assumes ownership.

A resource remains available within clear limits.

A rescuer says, "I will make this go away."

A resource says, "I will help you think through your options."

A rescuer acts before the other person engages.

A resource asks, "What have you tried?"

A rescuer repeatedly absorbs the consequence.

A resource may provide information, transportation, a one-time contribution, childcare during an appointment, or help locating professional support—without becoming the permanent solution.

Try replacing "What can I do to fix this?" with:

"What part of this can you handle?"

"What have you decided to do next?"

"Would you like me to listen, brainstorm, or help with one specific task?"

"Here is what I can offer. Does that help?"

"I cannot take this over, but I believe you can take the next step."

Becoming a resource allows your compassion to remain generous without making your life the emergency room for every person you love.

The Guilt of Putting the Bag Down

Release can feel wrong before it feels free.

You may feel guilty when you stop solving problems that others expect you to solve. You may feel selfish when you rest. You may question whether a boundary proves you do not love enough.

Guilt is not always evidence of wrongdoing.

Sometimes guilt is the emotional echo of an old role.

You were trained to keep everyone comfortable.

You were praised for never needing anything.

You learned that love meant self-erasure.

When you change the pattern, your emotions may lag behind your wisdom.

Do not make every decision based on which choice produces the least guilt today. Make it based on which choice creates the healthiest life over time.

The Release Ritual

Name the burden:

"I have been carrying responsibility for..."

Return it:

"This belongs to..."

Name your role:

"What belongs to me is..."

Choose your limit:

"I am willing to... I am not willing to..."

Then let your behavior match your words.

Release is rarely one dramatic moment. It is a series of smaller decisions not to pick the bag back up.

Remote Reset

Ask:

What am I carrying?

Who actually owns it?

What support can I offer without taking over?

What would I stop doing if I trusted this person to face their own life?

One Sentence to Carry

> *You can love people deeply without volunteering to become responsible for the life they choose.*

Chapter 6

Take Ownership of What Is

Release without ownership can become avoidance.

"That is not my problem" may sound freeing, but it can also become a way to escape necessary conversations, ignore your impact, or abandon responsibilities that are genuinely yours.

The ART Method does not remove responsibility. It puts responsibility in the right place.

After you accept what is and release what is not yours, you turn toward the most powerful question in the book:

What belongs to me now?

Responsibility Is Not Blame

Blame asks, "Whose fault is this?"

Responsibility asks, "What can I do from here?"

Blame looks for a target.

Responsibility looks for a choice.

You are not responsible for everything that has happened to you.

You are not responsible for another person's betrayal, abuse, discrimination, neglect, dishonesty, or immaturity.

You are not to blame for every wound you carry.

You are responsible for what you do with the power available to you now.

That may include getting help, telling the truth, grieving, leaving, documenting, reporting, apologizing, rebuilding, setting a limit, or choosing a new direction.

Ownership does not rewrite the past as your fault.

It refuses to let the past become the only author of your future.

Own Your Emotional Response Without Shaming It

People often say, "You made me angry," "You ruined my day," or "You made me feel worthless."

Other people can trigger real emotions. Their behavior may be harmful, unfair, or cruel. Emotional ownership does not deny that influence.

It recognizes that once an emotion is present, your relationship with that emotion belongs to you.

You can name it.

You can understand it.

You can regulate it.

You can decide what action it deserves.

You can seek support when it feels too large to manage alone.

Feelings are messengers. They are not always commanders.

Anger may tell you a boundary was crossed.

Fear may tell you safety or uncertainty needs attention.

Sadness may tell you something mattered.

Shame may reveal a wound—or a belief that needs to be challenged.

The goal is not to silence your emotions. It is to listen without surrendering the controls.

Own Your Contribution

Reclaiming your remote requires the courage to examine your own behavior.

Where have you avoided a conversation and then resented someone for not reading your mind?

Where have you said yes and secretly expected gratitude?

Where have you called control "help"?

Where have you stayed silent to keep the peace, then punished others with distance?

Where have you ignored evidence because the truth required a decision?

Ownership is not self-attack. It is self-honesty with a purpose.

You cannot change a pattern you are committed to defending.

A mature apology sounds like:

"I see what I did. I understand the impact. I am sorry. Here is what I will do differently."

It does not require you to take responsibility for the other person's entire response. It asks you to own your part cleanly.

Own Your Choices

A life is shaped by repeated choices more than occasional intentions.

You may intend to protect your peace, but continue answering every late-night call.

You may intend to value yourself, but keep negotiating with people who consistently devalue you.

You may intend to pursue a goal, but give every available hour to other people's emergencies.

Ownership closes the gap between what you say matters and what your choices reveal matters.

Ask:

What am I choosing through repetition?

What am I tolerating through inaction?

What am I postponing while waiting for permission?

What would change if I believed my life deserved my leadership?

Your choices may be constrained. They are not always unlimited. Money, health, caregiving, discrimination, legal obligations, and safety can narrow the options available.

Ownership does not pretend every person has equal power.

It asks you to use the power you do have honestly, strategically, and courageously.

Own Your Boundaries

A boundary is not a request for someone else to become different.

It is a decision about what you will do in response to what is happening.

Control says, "You need to stop speaking to me that way."

A boundary says, "If the conversation becomes insulting, I will end it and we can try again later."

Control says, "You cannot borrow money again."

A boundary says, "I am not available to lend more money."

Control says, "You have to respect my time."

A boundary says, "I will not continue changing my schedule for plans that are repeatedly canceled."

A boundary becomes real through your behavior.

You do not need the other person's agreement to keep a limit that governs your own participation.

Own the Next Right Step

When life feels overwhelming, the mind jumps to the entire future.

How will this relationship end?

What will everyone think?

What if I regret this?

How will I manage six months from now?

Ownership returns you to the next right step.

Not the perfect step.

Not the step that guarantees comfort.

The step that is honest, safe, aligned, and available now.

Make the appointment.

Send the application.

Write the budget.

Have the conversation.

Stop sending the message.

Ask for help.

Document the incident.

Take the walk.

Go to sleep before making the decision.

Your life is rarely reclaimed in one grand gesture. It returns through small choices that repeatedly place you back in your own hands.

Rebuilding Self-Trust

People who have handed away the remote often do not trust themselves.

They have made so many decisions by committee, approval, urgency, or fear that their own voice feels faint. When asked what they want, they first think about who might be disappointed.

Self-trust is not the belief that you will always choose correctly.

It is the belief that you will tell yourself the truth, make the best decision available, and remain present for the result.

You rebuild self-trust through evidence.

Keep Small Promises

Do what you said you would do for yourself.

Leave when you planned to leave.

Rest when the schedule says rest.

Make the call.

Do not send the message you decided was unwise.

Every kept promise tells your nervous system, *I do not disappear when someone else needs or wants something.*

Make Low-Stakes Decisions Without Polling

Choose the restaurant, clothing, schedule, class, or weekend plan without asking multiple people to confirm the choice.

Notice the urge to seek reassurance. Let the urge pass before you decide whether feedback is genuinely necessary.

Correct Without Condemning

When a decision does not work, do not use the outcome as proof that you should never trust yourself.

Ask:

What information did I have?

What did I miss?

What will I do differently?

What does this teach me about my values or limits?

Self-trust grows when mistakes become information rather than identity.

Stop Abandoning Yourself During Conflict

The moment another person becomes upset, stay connected to your own facts, values, and body.

You can listen.

You can reconsider.

You can apologize.

You can also maintain a decision.

Self-trust means you do not leave yourself merely because somebody else entered the room with a strong emotion.

Ownership and Repair

Sometimes the next right action is repair.

Perhaps you controlled because you were afraid. Perhaps you used guilt, silence, pressure, or repeated persuasion. Perhaps you set a limit harshly after months of saying nothing.

Ownership lets you apologize without surrendering the healthy decision underneath the poor delivery.

You might say:

"I was right to address the issue, and I was wrong in the way I spoke. I am sorry for raising my voice. The boundary itself remains important, and I would like to discuss it respectfully."

Or:

"I realize I kept offering advice after you said you wanted to decide for yourself. I am sorry. I will ask before giving input."

Repair is not humiliation. It is the practice of bringing your behavior back into alignment with your values.

The Ownership Plan

Complete the following:

The part I cannot control is...

The part I have been avoiding is...

My contribution to the pattern is...

The value I want to lead from is...

The boundary or action that belongs to me is...

The support I need is...

The next right step I will take within twenty-four hours is...

Remote Reset

When you feel powerless, ask:

What is not my fault?

What is still my responsibility?

What is one choice available to me now?

One Sentence to Carry

Ownership is not saying everything was your fault; it is deciding that your future will not be left unattended.

Chapter 7

Reclaim Your Remote in Relationships

Relationships are where the remote is easiest to lose.

Love makes us vulnerable. Attachment makes another person's behavior matter. History can turn a single sentence into a doorway to an old wound.

The goal is not to become unaffected by people you love. The goal is to remain connected without abandoning yourself.

Healthy relationships require two freedoms at once:

The other person is free to be who they are.

You are free to decide what that means for your participation.

Stop Dating Potential and Start Reading Patterns

Many people do not stay attached to the relationship they have. They stay attached to the relationship they believe could exist if the other person finally changed.

They date potential.

They parent potential.

They remain loyal to potential.

Potential can inspire hope, but patterns provide evidence.

Ask:

What happens consistently?

What changes after conflict?

Do apologies lead to repair?

Are my needs welcomed, negotiated, dismissed, or punished?

Can this person tolerate my boundaries?

Do I feel more like myself in this relationship—or less?

A relationship should not be judged by its best day alone. It should be understood by its repeated climate.

Love Without Controlling

Love can influence. It cannot own another person's will.

You may offer wisdom to a partner, guidance to a child, concern to a friend, or feedback to a family member.

Then comes the difficult part: letting the choice remain theirs.

Influence says, "Here is what I see."

Control says, "You must see it my way."

Influence says, "I care about what happens to you."

Control says, "I cannot be okay unless you choose what I think is best."

Influence leaves room for agency.

Control makes agreement the price of peace.

Loving without controlling does not mean staying close to every choice. You may love someone and decide not to finance the choice, cover for it, participate in it, or expose yourself to it.

You can honor their freedom and your own.

When Family Will Not Change

Family systems often assign roles early.

The responsible one.

The peacemaker.

The difficult one.

The successful one.

The one who never says no.

When you reclaim your remote, the system may resist—not because your boundary is wrong, but because your old role was convenient.

Someone may call you selfish when you stop being endlessly available.

Someone may say you have changed.

They may be right.

Growth changes your participation in familiar patterns.

You do not have to convince your family that your growth is good before you are allowed to continue growing.

A calm response may be:

"I understand this is different from what you are used to. It is still what I need to do."

Adult Children and the Pain of Watching

Few forms of release are harder than watching an adult child make a painful choice.

Parenthood trains you to protect, anticipate, and intervene. Adulthood requires a different posture.

You can remain loving without becoming the permanent manager of another adult's life.

You can offer support without erasing consequences.

You can communicate concern without repeating it until concern becomes pressure.

You can say:

"I love you. I see this differently. I trust that the decision is yours, and I am here to talk about what support I can realistically offer."

Release does not erase the ache. It keeps the ache from becoming control.

Where safety, dependency, disability, or legal responsibility is involved, the boundaries of responsibility may be different. Wisdom always considers the actual duty of care.

Friendships That Drain More Than They Give

Healthy friendship is not perfectly equal every day. Life has seasons. One person may need more during grief, illness, transition, or crisis.

Over time, however, healthy friendship contains mutual care, curiosity, respect, and effort.

A draining friendship may be one in which:

Every conversation becomes their emergency.

Your good news is minimized.

Your boundaries are treated as rejection.

You are expected to be available but cannot depend on them.

Conflict is avoided, weaponized, or never repaired.

You consistently leave contact feeling depleted, guilty, or small.

You do not have to make the other person a villain to change the level of access the relationship receives.

Some relationships need a conversation.

Some need a boundary.

Some need distance.

Some need an ending.

Acceptance helps you name which one.

Social Media and the Audience in Your Head

The remote can be handed to people you have never met.

A post performs poorly, and you question your value.

A stranger criticizes you, and your body carries the comment all day.

You compare your ordinary life to somebody else's edited moment.

You begin creating for approval instead of expression, service, or purpose.

Ask yourself:

Would I still believe this if no one applauded it?

Would I still choose this if nobody saw it?

Is this platform serving my values, or training my nervous system?

What deserves to be muted, unfollowed, limited, or removed?

Digital access is still access. Protect it accordingly.

Three Decisions Every Relationship Requires

When a relationship becomes painful, people often think they have only two options: tolerate everything or end everything.

Most relationships require three separate decisions.

Decision One: What Is True?

What is the actual pattern?

Not the best memory.

Not the worst argument.

Not the person's potential.

What happens over time?

Does the relationship contain honesty, care, effort, reciprocity, and repair? Are problems occasional and workable, or chronic and denied? Does the person take responsibility when harm is named?

Truth gives you a foundation.

Decision Two: What Level of Access Is Healthy?

Love and access are not identical.

A person may be important to you and still need limits around money, information, time, physical space, holidays, childcare, business, or emotional intimacy.

Access can be:

Frequent and close.

Warm but structured.

Limited to certain settings.

Temporarily paused.

Mediated through a professional or third party.

Ended for safety or well-being.

The right level is not determined by the title of the relationship alone. "Family" does not automatically mean unlimited access. "Friend" does not guarantee private information. "Partner" does not erase bodily, financial, or emotional boundaries.

Decision Three: What Work Is Mine?

You may need to communicate more clearly.

You may need to stop expecting mind-reading.

You may need to grieve.

You may need to apologize.

You may need to set and enforce a boundary.

You may need to stop making all the effort.

You may need professional support to decide safely.

The relationship's outcome is not entirely yours. Your participation is.

A Composite Relationship Example

Denise has a sister who calls frequently to criticize other family members and ask Denise to keep secrets. Denise dislikes the conversations but participates because she fears being labeled disloyal.

After each call, Denise feels tense and ashamed. She has tried changing the subject, but her sister returns to the same material.

Denise applies ART.

Accept: This is a repeated pattern, not an occasional difficult call. My sister may view gossip as closeness, and she may not agree with my limit.

Release: I release responsibility for preventing her anger and proving that I am a loyal sister by participating.

Take Ownership: I will say, "I want a relationship with you, but I am not willing to discuss family members who are not here. If the conversation returns to that, I will end the call and try again another day."

Her sister responds, "So now you think you are better than everyone?"

Denise does not defend her entire character. She replies, "No. I am telling you what I will participate in. We can talk about something else."

The sister continues, so Denise ends the call.

The boundary does not instantly improve the relationship. It improves Denise's participation in it.

That is often the first available form of change.

When Distance Is the Honest Choice

Distance should not be used to punish someone into chasing you. It may be appropriate when contact repeatedly causes harm, boundaries are ignored, repair is refused, or your safety and stability require space.

Distance can be temporary or ongoing. It can be quiet or explained. It can coexist with love, grief, prayer, and hope.

The question is not, "Will everyone understand?"

The question is, "What level of contact allows me to remain honest, safe, and whole?"

The Relationship Remote Check

Think of one relationship that occupies too much emotional space.

Accept:

What pattern is actually present?

Release:

What are you trying to make this person feel, understand, or choose?

Take Ownership:

What conversation, limit, decision, or grief belongs to you?

Then ask the most revealing question:

Who do I become when I am in this relationship?

The answer may tell you more than your explanations do.

Remote Reset

Use this script:

"I care about you. I cannot make this choice for you. What I can do is... What I cannot do is..."

One Sentence to Carry

Healthy love does not require you to disappear so someone else can remain comfortable.

Chapter 8

Reclaim Your Remote at Work

Work is more than a paycheck. It can become identity, status, security, purpose, and proof.

That is why a manager's opinion can feel larger than feedback. A missed promotion can feel like a verdict. A tense email can follow you home and sit at the dinner table.

You may not control workplace politics, difficult personalities, shifting priorities, or whether your contribution receives the recognition it deserves.

You can control the quality of your work, the clarity of your communication, the limits around your availability, the evidence you document, and the decisions you make about where you continue investing your talent.

Separate Feedback From Identity

Feedback can be useful without being absolute.

When criticism arrives, pause before deciding what it means about you.

Ask:

What specifically was said?

What evidence supports it?

What part is preference, and what part is performance?

Is there a useful correction here?

What does this source know—and what might they be missing?

A healthy response to feedback is neither automatic defensiveness nor automatic self-doubt.

It is discernment.

You can improve without agreeing that you are inadequate.

You can reject an unfair conclusion without rejecting every opportunity to grow.

Difficult Coworkers

Every workplace has people whose behavior pulls for a reaction.

The gossip.

The critic.

The chronic complainer.

The person who withholds information.

The colleague who creates a crisis, then recruits everyone else into it.

Reclaiming your remote does not mean pretending these behaviors do not affect the work. It means responding strategically instead of becoming emotionally organized around the person.

Keep communication factual.

Limit unnecessary exposure.

Clarify expectations in writing.

Address behavior rather than diagnosing character.

Document repeated concerns.

Escalate through appropriate channels when necessary.

Do not spend your entire evening conducting a trial in your head for a person who is not present.

Your coworker does not deserve unpaid office space in your mind.

Workplace Drama and the Cost of Attention

Drama survives on participation.

A rumor needs a listener.

An outrage needs repetition.

A conflict grows when everyone contributes an interpretation but no one contributes a direct conversation.

Before engaging, ask:

Does this involve me?

Do I have verified information?

Am I helping solve the problem—or helping circulate it?

Would I say this if the person were present?

What does professionalism require?

You do not have to attend every emotional meeting to which your workplace invites you.

Sometimes reclaiming your remote is changing the channel.

Managing Up Without Handing Over Your Worth

A supervisor has authority over aspects of your work. That does not make them the owner of your identity.

Clarify priorities when expectations compete.

Ask for measurable criteria.

Summarize decisions in writing.

Request feedback before the final deadline.

Bring solutions, not only frustration.

And notice when you are working for approval rather than effectiveness.

Approval-seeking at work often looks like:

Never saying no.

Overpreparing to avoid criticism.

Accepting work that belongs to others.

Staying silent when expectations are unclear.

Treating every correction as a threat.

Becoming indispensable can feel safe. It can also make exploitation easier.

Excellence and self-abandonment are not the same thing.

Leading Without Controlling

Leaders are especially vulnerable to the control illusion because outcomes matter and responsibility is real.

You can establish standards, assign responsibilities, provide feedback, remove obstacles, and hold people accountable.

You cannot force engagement, maturity, honesty, or motivation into another person.

Healthy leadership creates clarity and consequences. It does not attempt to micromanage another adult's internal world.

A strong leader asks:

Have I made the expectation clear?

Have I provided the needed resources?

Have I addressed the gap directly?

Have I documented and followed through?

Am I trying to coach a skill—or control a personality?

Leadership is influence plus accountability, not anxiety disguised as supervision.

When the Workplace Is Harmful

Some problems are not mindset problems.

Harassment, discrimination, retaliation, unsafe conditions, wage violations, bullying, and unethical conduct may require documentation, formal reporting, legal guidance, union or human-resources support, or an exit plan.

Do not use "protect your peace" to minimize conduct that should be addressed.

Reclaiming your remote may mean refusing to normalize what is harmful.

It may mean building a record.

It may mean asking for accommodations.

It may mean seeking counsel.

It may mean leaving strategically rather than enduring indefinitely.

Your peace matters, and so do your rights.

A Week in a Difficult Workplace

Consider a composite workplace scenario.

Andre is capable and respected, but his supervisor frequently changes priorities without adjusting deadlines. When projects are delayed, the supervisor questions Andre's organization in front of the team.

Andre's old pattern is to work late, absorb the added task, and hope his effort will prevent criticism. He does not ask which priority should move because he fears appearing uncooperative.

By Thursday, he is angry with everyone—including colleagues who did not create the problem.

ART helps him separate the situation.

Accept

The supervisor is changing priorities.

The current workload cannot be completed at the expected quality within the existing hours.

Andre has been saying yes without documenting the tradeoff.

The supervisor may respond defensively when asked to prioritize.

Release

Andre releases responsibility for making an impossible workload look possible.

He releases the belief that professionalism requires silent overextension.

He releases control over whether his supervisor likes the clarification.

Take Ownership

Andre creates a written list of current projects, deadlines, and estimated hours. When the next urgent request arrives, he replies:

"I can begin this today. I am currently scheduled to complete the client report and budget review by Friday. Based on the time available, one of those will need to move. Please confirm the priority order."

He also follows meetings with brief written summaries:

"To confirm today's decision, I will pause the budget review and complete the client revision first. The budget review will move to Tuesday."

Andre does not become combative. He becomes visible.

If the pattern continues, he now has documentation for a higher-level conversation, human-resources consultation, workload adjustment, or job search.

What Professional Boundaries Protect

Professional boundaries do not only protect comfort. They protect accuracy, ethics, safety, and quality.

A nurse who never speaks about unsafe staffing is not protecting the team.

An educator who absorbs every unassigned duty may conceal a systemic capacity problem.

A leader who refuses to delegate may prevent others from developing.

An employee who works off the clock may make an unrealistic process appear sustainable.

Boundaries reveal the true cost of work.

They allow organizations to make decisions using accurate information rather than invisible sacrifice.

The Workday Decompression Practice

Before leaving work—or before entering your home if you work remotely—take five minutes.

Write:

What happened today?

What needs action tomorrow?

What is documented?

What am I tempted to replay tonight?

What belongs to someone else's role?

What evidence do I have that I did enough for one day?

Then complete one physical action that marks transition: close the laptop, change clothes, walk around the block, wash your hands, play one song, or take three slow breaths before entering the next part of your life.

Your body needs a signal that the channel has changed.

Scripts for the Workday

"I can complete A or B by Friday. Which is the higher priority?"

"I want to make sure I understand the expectation. What would a successful outcome look like?"

"I am available to discuss the project. I am not willing to continue the conversation while being spoken to disrespectfully."

"Please send that request by email so I can track the details and deadline."

"I am not the right owner for that task. The appropriate contact is..."

"I need time to review this feedback before I respond."

Professional does not mean powerless.

Remote Reset

At the end of the workday, ask:

What belongs to the job?

What belongs to me?

What am I taking home that can stay here?

What needs action, documentation, or release tomorrow?

One Sentence to Carry

Your job may evaluate your performance; it does not get to define your worth.

Chapter 9

Boundaries Without Guilt

A boundary is a line that protects what matters.

Your time.

Your body.

Your money.

Your attention.

Your emotional energy.

Your values.

Your safety.

Your capacity to love without resentment.

Many people wait to set boundaries until they are furious. By then, the boundary arrives as an explosion rather than a clear decision.

Healthy boundaries are not punishments delivered after depletion. They are information offered before resentment becomes the only language left.

Boundaries and Control

Control tells another person what they must do.

A boundary explains what you will do.

Control: "You cannot call me after 10:00 p.m."

Boundary: "I silence my phone at 10:00 p.m. and respond the next day."

Control: "You need to stop bringing up my past."

Boundary: "If my past is used to insult me, I will end the conversation."

Control: "You must agree with my parenting."

Boundary: "I am willing to discuss concerns respectfully. I am not willing to debate my decisions in front of my child."

The distinction is not merely wording. A boundary is something you have the power and willingness to carry out.

A threat tries to frighten someone into compliance.

A boundary prepares you to act in alignment with your values.

The Anatomy of a Clear Boundary

A practical boundary has four parts:

The situation: What is happening?

The limit: What is or is not acceptable to you?

The action: What will you do if it continues?

The consistency: Are you prepared to follow through?

For example:

"When plans are canceled at the last minute repeatedly, it disrupts my schedule. Going forward, I will not rearrange other commitments until plans are confirmed the day before."

You do not need a courtroom argument. You need clarity.

Why Boundaries Create Guilt

Boundaries can feel unkind when your identity has been built around access.

You may believe a good person always answers.

A loving parent always rescues.

A loyal friend never disappoints.

A committed employee is always available.

A faithful person never says no.

These beliefs turn generosity into obligation and obligation into resentment.

A boundary may disappoint someone. Disappointment is not the same as harm.

A boundary may change a relationship. Change is not always failure.

A boundary may reveal that a relationship depended on your lack of one.

That revelation can hurt, but it is useful information.

Pushback Does Not Automatically Mean the Boundary Is Wrong

People who benefited from your overextension may experience your balance as deprivation.

They may argue.

They may guilt you.

They may test the limit.

They may become unusually charming, unusually angry, or suddenly helpless.

Do not evaluate a boundary only by the first reaction it receives.

Evaluate it by its alignment with your values, your actual capacity, the health of the relationship, and the pattern it is designed to address.

Listen for valid feedback. Adjust when wisdom calls for adjustment. Do not abandon a necessary limit merely because someone dislikes it.

Boundaries Across Your Life

Time boundaries protect your schedule and rest.

Emotional boundaries separate empathy from emotional absorption.

Financial boundaries define what you will give, lend, pay, or guarantee.

Digital boundaries govern access through phones, messages, email, and social media.

Physical boundaries protect your body, space, privacy, and safety.

Conversational boundaries define what topics, tones, and forms of communication you will participate in.

Work boundaries protect role clarity, availability, and fair distribution of responsibility.

Spiritual boundaries protect conscience and prevent faith from being used to coerce, shame, or silence.

You may need different boundaries with different people. Equal love does not require equal access.

The Boundary Ladder

Not every problem requires the strongest response first. A boundary ladder helps you respond proportionately while noticing whether the other person is willing to cooperate.

Step One: Name the Need

Begin with a clear request when a request is appropriate.

"Please let me know by Thursday whether you are attending."

"I need you to ask before sharing my personal information."

"Please speak to me directly rather than through another family member."

A request gives the relationship an opportunity to respond without consequence language.

Step Two: Clarify the Limit

If the pattern continues, explain what does not work and what you will do.

"I need confirmation by Thursday. If I do not receive it, I will plan without you."

"I am not comfortable with my information being shared. If it happens again, I will be more selective about what I discuss."

"I will not participate in conversations carried through other people. You can contact me directly."

Step Three: Reduce Access or Participation

When the limit is ignored, change your behavior.

Stop rearranging the schedule.

Share less information.

End the call.

Leave the gathering.

Move communication to writing.

Decline the next request.

A boundary without behavior becomes a suggestion.

Step Four: Seek Structure or Support

Some patterns require mediation, counseling, supervision, human resources, legal advice, medical guidance, financial safeguards, or a formal safety plan.

Outside structure is not failure. It may be the most responsible response when private conversation has not created change.

Step Five: Reconsider the Relationship or Environment

If the behavior remains harmful and the person consistently rejects accountability, you may need greater distance, a role change, financial separation, relocation, resignation, or an ending.

The ladder is not a rigid rule. Danger may require immediate movement to safety rather than gradual escalation. The purpose is to help you see that boundaries can develop through increasingly protective actions.

Boundary Consequences Are Not Revenge

A consequence is the predictable result of a limit.

If the conversation becomes abusive, the call ends.

If payment is not received, the service pauses.

If plans are not confirmed, the time is released.

If trust is repeatedly broken, access changes.

Revenge seeks to cause pain.

A consequence seeks to protect what the boundary names.

Before choosing a consequence, ask:

Does this action protect the value or resource involved?

Is it proportionate to the pattern?

Am I willing and able to carry it out?

Would I make the same choice if the other person never apologized?

Am I trying to create safety—or force remorse?

The cleanest consequence is one you can implement without drama, threats, or repeated warnings.

Boundaries With Yourself

Some of the most important boundaries are internal.

I will not check the message again tonight.

I will wait twenty-four hours before lending money.

I will not discuss private conflict while angry.

I will leave the app after thirty minutes.

I will not volunteer until I review my calendar.

I will not make a permanent decision to escape a temporary emotion.

A boundary with yourself protects you from the version of you that seeks immediate relief at the cost of long-term peace.

The Broken-Record Method

People-pleasers often weaken a boundary by overexplaining it.

Use a brief statement. Repeat it calmly.

"I understand you are disappointed. I am still not available."

"I have answered the question. My decision has not changed."

"I am willing to talk when we can do so respectfully."

"That does not work for me."

"I will not discuss this in front of the children."

"I am not able to lend money."

The goal is not to win agreement. It is to communicate and maintain the limit.

Boundaries and Safety

In coercive, abusive, or dangerous relationships, direct boundary-setting may increase risk. A person who seeks control may not respond to ordinary communication in ordinary ways.

Safety planning may require confidential support, professional guidance, legal protection, emergency services, or assistance from a domestic-violence organization. Do not announce a boundary or exit plan when doing so could place you or someone else in greater danger.

A safe boundary is not always a spoken sentence. Sometimes it is a protected plan.

The Boundary Test

Ask:

Where do I repeatedly feel resentment?

Where do I say yes while my body says no?

What behavior do I keep tolerating because I fear the reaction to a limit?

Who has access to me without regard for my capacity?

What am I expecting another person to stop doing when I need to decide what I will do?

What boundary would allow me to remain loving without becoming depleted?

Remote Reset

Use this formula:

"When ___ happens, I will ___. I am available for ___. I am not available for ___."

One Sentence to Carry

> *A boundary is not a wall around your heart; it is a door you are responsible for opening wisely.*

Chapter 10

Keep the Remote: Living Free

You will hand the remote away again.

A comment will catch you on a tired day.

A person you love will make a choice that frightens you.

An old family role will invite you back.

A workplace conflict will follow you home.

You will overexplain, overthink, overfunction, or say yes before you check your capacity.

This does not mean you failed.

Freedom is not a permanent emotional state. It is the practice of returning.

Again and again, you notice who or what has taken over your attention. Again and again, you bring yourself back to reality, responsibility, and choice.

The Buttons on Your Remote

The metaphor becomes most useful when you turn it into daily behavior.

PAUSE

A pause creates space between activation and action.

Before you send the message, volunteer the money, agree to the request, or make the accusation, stop long enough to ask:

What am I feeling?

What story am I telling?

What outcome am I trying to control?

What would a wise response look like after I sleep, breathe, pray, walk, or gather more information?

A pause is not avoidance when it prepares you to respond better.

MUTE

Not every opinion deserves equal volume.

Mute the group chat that keeps you activated.

Mute the account that turns inspiration into inadequacy.

Mute the inner voice that confuses one mistake with your entire identity.

Mute commentary from people who do not carry the consequences of your decisions.

Silence is not always denial. Sometimes it is stewardship of attention.

REWIND

Rewind to learn, not to relive.

Ask what happened, what you missed, what you would do differently, and what the moment revealed.

Then stop using reflection as a form of self-punishment.

The past should become a teacher, not a room where you live.

FAST-FORWARD

When a choice feels good in the moment, fast-forward to its likely consequence.

If I say yes from guilt, how will I feel next week?

If I rescue again, what pattern will I reinforce?

If I avoid this conversation, what will the silence cost?

If I respond publicly while angry, what will I have to repair?

Wisdom considers more than immediate relief.

VOLUME

Whatever receives repeated attention becomes louder.

You can amplify fear, resentment, criticism, and comparison.

You can also amplify truth, gratitude, support, purpose, and the evidence of your growth.

This is not pretending pain does not exist. It is refusing to let pain become the only sound in the room.

CHANNEL

Attention is a channel.

You may not control what appears, but you have influence over what you continue watching.

Change the channel from their choices to your values.

From the conversation you cannot change to the action you can take.

From imagined judgment to present responsibility.

From proving yourself to becoming yourself.

POWER

The power button is not power over other people.

It is the authority to choose your participation.

To speak.

To stop.

To leave.

To stay and work.

To ask for help.

To begin again.

To refuse access.

To offer grace without abandoning wisdom.

The power is not that you can control everything.

The power is that everything does not get to control you.

Your Daily Remote Check

At the beginning or end of each day, ask:

Who or what held too much of my attention today?

What emotion did I need to feel rather than fix?

What did I carry that belongs to someone else?

What responsibility did I avoid that belongs to me?

Where did I honor a boundary?

What is one choice I am proud of?

What do I need to accept, release, and own tomorrow?

Five honest minutes can interrupt a pattern that has been running for years.

When You Slip Back Into an Old Role

Old roles feel familiar, and familiarity can feel like safety.

You may return to rescuing because being needed makes you feel valuable.

You may return to people-pleasing because disapproval still activates fear.

You may return to control because uncertainty feels unbearable.

Do not shame yourself. Get curious.

What need was the old pattern trying to meet?

Safety?

Belonging?

Worth?

Predictability?

Connection?

Then ask how you can meet that need without surrendering your remote.

You may need reassurance from a trusted person, a clearer plan, professional support, prayer, rest, information, or a boundary you have been postponing.

Compassion makes change more sustainable than contempt.

A Seven-Day Remote Reset

Day One: Notice. Record every moment another person's behavior changes your emotional direction.

Day Two: Separate. Divide a page into "Mine" and "Not Mine."

Day Three: Accept. Name one reality you have been resisting.

Day Four: Release. Stop one rescuing, overexplaining, or approval-seeking behavior.

Day Five: Own. Take one action you have delayed while focusing on someone else.

Day Six: Bound. Communicate or implement one clear limit.

Day Seven: Return. Review what changed in your energy, relationships, and thinking.

Then begin again—not because you failed to finish, but because freedom is practiced in cycles.

A Thirty-Day Reclaiming Practice

Lasting change needs repetition. Use the following four-week practice to move ART from an idea into a pattern.

Week One: Awareness

The goal of Week One is not to change everything. It is to notice accurately.

Each day, record one moment when your mood, behavior, or self-worth became organized around another person's reaction.

Write:

What happened?

What button was pressed—approval, guilt, urgency, rejection, comparison, conflict, or rescue?

What did I feel in my body?

What did I do automatically?

What was I trying to prevent?

At the end of the week, circle the button that appears most often. That is your primary training ground.

Week Two: Separation

The goal of Week Two is to sort responsibility.

For each difficult situation, make two lists:

Mine: my words, behavior, preparation, boundaries, choices, repair, and support.

Not Mine: another adult's choice, private thought, reaction, timing, effort, lesson, and outcome.

Pay attention to items you keep placing in both columns. That confusion is often where anxiety lives.

Practice saying:

"I can influence this, but I cannot guarantee it."

"I can care about this without carrying it."

"Their feeling matters, and it still belongs to them."

Week Three: Action

The goal of Week Three is to choose one behavior that keeps the remote in your hands.

Pause before answering.

Ask before giving advice.

Let a nonurgent message wait.

State one preference.

Allow someone to solve a problem you usually take over.

Communicate a small boundary.

Make one decision without polling.

Take one step toward a goal that has been delayed by other people's emergencies.

Do not choose the hardest possible action simply to prove courage. Choose an action small enough to repeat.

Week Four: Integration

The goal of Week Four is to practice ART during a real emotional moment.

When activated, write or say:

Accept: The truth is...

Release: I am not responsible for...

Take Ownership: The next right action is...

At the end of the day, ask:

Did I act from values or from urgency?

Did I communicate or attempt to control?

Did I support or rescue?

Did I remain connected to myself during someone else's emotion?

What needs repair?

What deserves recognition?

Measuring Progress Differently

Do not measure progress only by whether other people respond well.

A boundary may be successful even when someone dislikes it.

A conversation may be successful even without agreement.

Release may be successful even while grief remains.

Ownership may be successful even when the outcome is uncertain.

Measure progress by questions such as:

Did I tell the truth sooner?

Did I spend less time rehearsing?

Did I recover more quickly after criticism?

Did I ask what support was wanted before taking over?

Did I notice guilt without obeying it?

Did I keep one promise to myself?

Did I make a decision from values rather than fear?

Freedom often appears first as a shorter recovery time, a clearer sentence, or a pause where an automatic yes used to be.

Small evidence matters.

Build Your Remote Team

Self-leadership does not mean isolation.

Identify people who help you keep the remote rather than take it from you.

A healthy support person does not make every decision for you. They ask questions that return you to your own values.

They can validate your feelings without escalating every conflict.

They can challenge you without shaming you.

They can remind you of patterns when fear makes you forget.

Your team may include a trusted friend, counselor, coach, pastor, mentor, support group, physician, attorney, financial professional, or workplace advocate, depending on the situation.

Ask for the kind of support you need:

"Please listen without solving."

"Help me separate the facts from my fear."

"Remind me what I said my boundary would be."

"I need professional guidance before I act."

"Please check on me after the conversation."

Reclaiming your remote is personal work. It does not have to be lonely work.

The Legacy of Emotional Leadership

When you reclaim your remote, the benefit extends beyond you.

Children learn that love does not require emotional enmeshment.

Friends experience support without control.

Teams experience leadership without anxiety.

Family members encounter honesty without manipulation.

You model that boundaries and compassion can coexist.

You teach people how to relate to you, and you give them permission to take responsibility for themselves.

Not everyone will welcome the change.

Some relationships may deepen.

Some may become more honest.

Some may reveal that they were sustained by your overfunctioning.

Whatever the result, you will be living from truth rather than fear.

That is freedom.

Remote Reset

Finish each line:

Today I will pause before...

Today I will mute...

Today I will stop rewinding...

Today I will change the channel from... to...

Today I will use my power to...

One Sentence to Carry

Freedom is not never losing your remote; it is becoming skilled at returning it to your own hands.

Conclusion

Your Life Is Back in Your Hands

At the beginning of this book, you were invited to imagine your life with a remote control.

Perhaps you recognized how often you had handed it away.

To a parent whose approval you were still chasing.

To a partner whose mood determined the climate of your day.

To an adult child whose choices kept you awake.

To a workplace that confused performance with worth.

To an audience that could applaud you on Monday and ignore you on Tuesday.

To a past that kept pressing REWIND.

You may have believed that caring required carrying.

That love required control.

That peace would arrive when everybody finally behaved differently.

Now you know another way.

Accept what is true.

Release what does not belong to you.

Take Ownership of what does.

ART will not make people predictable.

It will not prevent disappointment.

It will not remove grief, conflict, uncertainty, or the need for difficult decisions.

It will return you to the place where your real power has always lived:

Your response.

Your values.

Your boundaries.

Your choices.

Your next right step.

You were never meant to manage every life around you.

You were never meant to trade your peace for universal approval.

You were never meant to keep proving your love by abandoning yourself.

You were meant to lead your life.

Not perfectly.

Honestly.

Courageously.

One pause.

One boundary.

One decision.

One day at a time.

The remote is yours.

Keep it.

And live free.

Appendix A

ART in Sixty Seconds

When you feel emotionally hijacked, use this one-minute reset.

1. ACCEPT

Name the fact without adding a verdict.

"The truth is..."

Examples:

The truth is that they said no.

The truth is that I do not know what they are thinking.

The truth is that this pattern has happened more than once.

The truth is that I am disappointed.

2. RELEASE

Name what is not yours to carry or control.

"I release responsibility for..."

Examples:

Their approval.

Their reaction to my respectful boundary.

The lesson they choose to learn.

The outcome I cannot guarantee.

3. TAKE OWNERSHIP

Choose the next action that belongs to you.

"My next right step is..."

Examples:

Ask one clarifying question.

End the disrespectful conversation.

Wait until tomorrow to respond.

Apologize for my part.

Document the concern.

Rest.

Seek support.

The Pocket Version

What is true? What is not mine? What will I do next?

Appendix B

Boundary Scripts

Use these as starting points. Adjust the language to fit your voice, culture, relationship, and safety needs.

Time and Availability

"I am not available tonight. I can talk tomorrow between 6:00 and 6:30."

"I need advance notice before I commit."

"I am not able to take that on."

"I can help for one hour, and then I need to leave."

"I do not respond to nonurgent messages after 9:00 p.m."

Family

"I understand that you disagree. I am not discussing this decision again."

"I love you, and I am not able to solve this for you."

"I am willing to listen. I am not willing to be yelled at."

"I will not participate in conversations that criticize another family member who is not present."

"I am not keeping this secret when someone's safety is involved."

Money

"I am not able to lend money."

"I can contribute $___ one time. I cannot commit to ongoing support."

"I do not cosign loans."

"I am willing to help you review a budget. I am not able to pay the bill."

"I need repayment terms in writing before I agree."

Work

"Which current priority should move if this new task becomes urgent?"

"I am available during my scheduled hours."

"Please include me on the email so expectations are documented."

"I can discuss the feedback. I will not continue the conversation while being insulted."

"That task falls outside my role. Who is the appropriate owner?"

Friendship and Dating

"I value our relationship, and I need more consistency than this pattern provides."

"I am not comfortable continuing a conversation that becomes disrespectful."

"I am not ready to make that commitment."

"I need time to think before I answer."

"I care about you. I am not available to be your only source of support."

Digital Boundaries

"I do not discuss private conflict on social media."

"I am stepping away from this group chat."

"I will respond when I have the capacity."

"Please do not post photos of me without asking."

"I am muting notifications so I can focus."

When Someone Pushes Back

"I hear that you are disappointed. My answer is still no."

"You do not have to agree with my boundary for me to keep it."

"I have explained what I can offer."

"This is not a punishment. It is the limit I need."

"We can revisit the conversation when we are both calm."

Appendix C

Book Club and Group Discussion Guide

1. Who or what most often gets access to your emotional remote?
2. Where did you first learn that love meant keeping other people happy?
3. What is the difference between being affected by someone and being directed by them?
4. Which is most difficult for you: Accept, Release, or Take Ownership? Why?
5. What reality have you been resisting because accepting it would require a decision?
6. Where have you confused caring with carrying?
7. What silent contract may be operating in one of your relationships?
8. How can rescuing interfere with another person's growth?
9. What emotion are you tempted to treat as instruction rather than information?
10. What part of your current situation is not your fault but is now your responsibility to address?
11. What pattern in a relationship have you minimized because of the person's potential?
12. How do family roles make it difficult to change?
13. What does healthy influence look like in parenting, partnership, friendship, or leadership?
14. Where does workplace approval have too much power over your self-worth?
15. Which type of boundary—time, emotional, financial, digital, physical, conversational, work, or spiritual—needs the most attention?
16. How does guilt show up when you set a limit?
17. What is the difference between a boundary and a threat?
18. Which remote-control button—Pause, Mute, Rewind, Fast-Forward, Volume, Channel, or Power—would most improve your life right now?

19. What is one burden you are ready to return to its rightful owner?
20. What is one next right step you will take within twenty-four hours?

Group Practice

Invite each person to complete this three-part statement: **Accept:** The truth I am willing to face is... **Release:** The burden I am willing to put down is... **Take Ownership:** The action I am willing to take is... Close by asking each person to name one sentence from the book they want to carry into the coming week.

Appendix D

Who's Holding Your Remote? Self-Assessment

Rate each statement from 0 to 3:

- **0 — Rarely**
- **1 — Sometimes**
- **2 — Often**
- **3 — Almost always**

1. My mood changes quickly when someone important to me seems upset.
2. I replay criticism long after the conversation ends.
3. I feel responsible for preventing the people I love from making mistakes.
4. I say yes before checking my time, energy, or finances.
5. I overexplain decisions when someone disagrees.
6. I have difficulty resting while someone close to me has a problem.
7. I monitor text messages, facial expressions, or tone for signs of rejection.
8. I feel guilty when I allow another adult to experience consequences.
9. I ask several people for opinions before making ordinary decisions.
10. I become resentful after doing things I volunteered to do.
11. I believe a good parent, partner, friend, leader, or family member should always be available.
12. I take criticism as evidence about my worth rather than information about one behavior or result.
13. I repeat advice after the other person has heard and declined it.
14. I lose sleep over choices that belong to another adult.
15. I postpone my own goals because other people's needs always feel more urgent.
16. I feel rejected when someone does not use the help I offered.
17. I remain in conversations after the tone becomes disrespectful.

18. I believe peace will come when a particular person finally changes.
19. I cover, explain, pay, or fix in ways that protect a recurring pattern.
20. I confuse another person's disappointment with proof that I have done something wrong.
21. I find it difficult to name what I want without first considering everyone else's preference.
22. I worry that boundaries will make me selfish or unloving.
23. I stay emotionally activated by social-media reactions, comparison, or silence.
24. I take workplace problems home mentally even when no action can be taken that evening.
25. I feel valuable mainly when I am needed.

Scoring

Add your responses.

0–18: The Remote Is Mostly in Your Hands

You may still have specific triggers, but you generally distinguish your responsibility from other people's. Focus on the items you scored 2 or 3; those are the situations where an old pattern may still operate.

19–37: The Remote Changes Hands Under Stress

You likely function well until conflict, guilt, rejection, urgency, or uncertainty appears. Your work is to identify the button most likely to trigger an automatic response and build a pause around it.

38–56: You Are Carrying More Than Your Share

Over-responsibility may be affecting your energy, relationships, finances, rest, or self-trust. Practice the ART Method with one recurring pattern rather than attempting to change every relationship at once.

57–75: Your Emotional Life May Be Organized Around Other People

The patterns described in this book may be deeply connected to identity, family roles, fear, trauma, or long-standing relationship dynamics. Consider using the book alongside qualified professional support. Seeking help is not giving away the remote; it is choosing resources that strengthen your ability to lead your life.

This assessment is a reflection tool, not a diagnosis.

Your Results

My total score is...

The five statements I scored highest are...

The button beneath those statements is usually...

The relationship or setting where this pattern is strongest is...

The cost of the pattern has been...

The need I have been trying to meet is...

The first ART practice I will use is...

Appendix E

Thirty Days of Remote Reset Journal Prompts

Day 1 – Notice the Transfer

Who or what had the greatest influence over your mood today? What happened inside you before you reacted?

Day 2 – Name the Button

Which button is easiest to press: approval, guilt, urgency, rejection, comparison, conflict, or rescue? Where did you learn to respond that way?

Day 3 – Separate Fact From Story

Describe one recent event. What are the verified facts? What story did you tell about what those facts meant?

Day 4 – Find the Fear

What are you afraid would happen if you stopped managing this person, relationship, or outcome?

Day 5 – Identify the Reward

What does overfunctioning give you—certainty, praise, usefulness, closeness, avoidance, or a sense of control?

Day 6 – Audit Your Yes

Review three recent yeses. Which were freely chosen? Which were given from guilt, fear, or urgency?

Day 7 – Practice a Pause

Where could a ten-minute, one-hour, or overnight pause improve your next response?

Day 8 – Accept One Fact

What truth have you been softening, minimizing, or calling temporary despite repeated evidence?

Day 9 – Grieve the Hope

What version of a person, relationship, or future have you been waiting for? What would it mean to honor the hope and live in today's reality?

Day 10 – Believe the Pattern

What has consistent behavior shown you that words alone have not?

Day 11 – Name What Is Not Yours

List five choices, feelings, lessons, or outcomes that belong to other adults.

Day 12 – Return the Emotion

Whose disappointment, anger, anxiety, or sadness have you adopted? How can you remain compassionate without taking it over?

Day 13 – Cancel a Silent Contract

Where have you overgiven while silently expecting gratitude, loyalty, agreement, or change?

Day 14 – Stop One Rescue

What is one task, consequence, or problem you can allow an able adult to handle?

Day 15 – Become a Resource

How can you offer limited, specific support without becoming the solution?

Day 16 – Name What Is Yours

What conversation, decision, apology, boundary, or act of care belongs to you now?

Day 17 – Own Your Contribution

Without blaming yourself for everything, what behavior of yours has helped keep a painful pattern in place?

Day 18 – Repair Cleanly

Is there an apology you owe? Write it without excuses, self-condemnation, or an expectation that forgiveness must be immediate.

Day 19 – Keep a Promise to Yourself

What small promise will you keep today to strengthen self-trust?

Day 20 – Decide Without Polling

What low-stakes decision can you make without seeking multiple opinions?

Day 21 – Read the Relationship Climate

Choose one relationship. What is its repeated climate? Who do you become inside it?

Day 22 – Adjust Access

Does someone have more access to your time, money, information, body, or emotional energy than is healthy?

Day 23 – State a Preference

What do you want, need, prefer, or believe? Write it before considering how others may react.

Day 24 – Build a Boundary

Complete: "When ___ happens, I will ___. I am available for ___. I am not available for ___."

Day 25 – Prepare for Pushback

What response do you fear after setting the boundary? What calm sentence can you repeat?

Day 26 — Protect the Workday

What workplace issue needs action or documentation? What work stress can remain at work tonight?

Day 27 — Use the Buttons

Which button do you need today: Pause, Mute, Rewind, Fast-Forward, Volume, Channel, or Power? What action represents pressing it?

Day 28 — Measure Real Progress

Where did you recover faster, speak sooner, explain less, rescue less, or stay connected to yourself?

Day 29 — Choose Your Remote Team

Who helps you become clearer rather than more reactive? What specific support can you request?

Day 30 — Write Your Remote Declaration

Complete:

I accept...

I release...

I take ownership of...

I will no longer trade my peace for...

I will protect...

When I hand the remote away, I will return to...

The life I am ready to lead is...

About the Author

Yvette W. Johnson, Ed.D. is an educator, counselor, entrepreneur, author, and advocate for emotional wellness and personal growth. Her professional experience across education, school counseling, leadership, and educational diagnosis has given her a practical view of how people respond to pressure, relationships, responsibility, and change.

Dr. Johnson created the ART Method—Accept, Release, and Take Ownership—to help people distinguish caring from carrying, influence from control, and responsibility from blame. Her work equips readers to establish healthier boundaries, protect their peace, and lead their lives with greater clarity and courage.

Through her writing, teaching, and community work, Dr. Johnson reminds people that freedom does not begin when everyone else changes. It begins when they stop handing away the authority to direct their own lives.

www.ingramcontent.com/pod-product-compliance
Lightning Source LLC
LaVergne TN
LVHW030728061126
851857LV00019B/2030
* 9 7 9 8 9 9 6 5 2 9 4 1 4 *